Prison without Bars

Prison without Bars

It Starts Within

CARLOS M CHRISTIAN

ISBN: 1515375951
ISBN 13: 9781515375951
Library of Congress Control Number: 2015912810
CreateSpace Independent Publishing Platform
North Charleston, South Carolina

Introduction

I HAVE FIGURED OUT that finding yourself in prison serving multiple years for crimes you committed is not the worst thing that can happen. What is worse is serving those years in a place you consider right next door to hell and wanting from the depths of your soul to go home and be around people you love so you can live life in a manner that contradicts the hell you are currently experiencing. When what you want so badly finally arrives and you're presented the opportunity to go home but you are not properly prepared to make that transition back into society, you squander the opportunity and become a recidivist. Then you go back into that same hell at a later date as an older individual and get sentenced to another prison term! That has to be the worst, but it happens so often in the US penal system nationwide that it's disturbing. It is also very expensive, with the cost of each recidivist totaling $94,856 with an average stay of three to six years.

The prison system was a different culture in the early years of its conception. In those days, it provided little to no assistance for individuals who had to return to their communities. But now, with so much attention on this problem from governmental agencies and lawmakers, the approach has shifted. With millions of dollars funneled into reentry programs across the nation from local businesses, federal grants, and private donors, it is much more feasible for someone who has been incarcerated to successfully transition back into society.

I was incarcerated at nineteen years old to serve a ten-year prison sentence as a first-time offender. I had to adapt to a culture, and it was truly a culture shock. I had a three-month-old son when I was incarcerated, and all I ever wanted to do was provide for my son and be a good father. I sold drugs to accomplish this goal, and as a result, I received time in a state prison, where I only saw my son four times a year, maybe five if I was lucky. This was more visitation time than most had, so I wasn't complaining. I was able to transition back into society and secure employment, get married, gain custody of my son, purchase a house in a suburban area, and make a tremendous impact in the reentry community with the organization my wife and I cofounded, the Starts Within Organization in Columbus, Ohio.

I realized it was possible for my story to be duplicated by others currently going through what I went through. Anyone can be productive and enjoy life in a way that I always knew was possible, but I just did not have the right approach to be successful. I turned prison into a training ground and made my ten-year incarceration the foundation of my current success as a restored citizen.

Prison without Bars is written to give hope to people who are affected by this epidemic of incarceration that plagues communities and households across the nation. This book explains the recipe for surviving prison and going on to live in a way that brings quality to your own life and the lives of people you touch.

During my ten years, the only thing I saw was people recidivating within one to three years and along with that came the discouraging stories of how bad it was. The chances of you avoiding recidivism was almost impossible were the common stories that were told. I studied those individuals who failed, and I started to see commonality in them all. I utilized my understanding to do differently than they did.

Prison without Bars gives you an inside look at what it takes to be successful during and after prison. This is not a book to discuss the problem, say how bad it is, and set up a march or a protest without providing the solution to overcome the problem. One of the biggest mistakes incarcerated people make is believing that it is everybody else who has to come in alignment in pushing for their success for them to be successful, and that is the furthest from the truth. It puts you in the hands of somebody else not as invested in your success as you are.

The decision to be successful after prison is yours. There are many challenges, but the greatest challenge anyone faces is the challenge of oneself. An ancient African proverb reads, "If there is no enemy within, the enemy outside can do us no harm." Change is not a simple task, but it is mandatory that you embrace change in order to be successful during and after prison.

1

The State of Incarceration

*R*ECIDIVISM IS A word that gets butchered in its pronunciation by so many individuals despite education level and effective speaking abilities. It refers to a person's relapse into criminal behavior, often after that person receives sanctions or undergoes intervention for a previous crime. Simply put, recidivism is getting released from prison, getting back into the same lifestyle that got someone incarcerated in the first place, committing another crime, and having to return to prison to do another prison term. Individuals being monitored to see if they become recidivist find it very simple to go back to prison once released.

A study released by the Bureau of Justice Statistics provided information for recidivism in 2014. The study tracked 404,638 state prisoners, all of whom were released in 2005, from thirty states. It found that 67.8 percent of them were rearrested within three years of their release, and 76.6 percent were rearrested within five years. Of the latter group, more than a third were rearrested in the first six months after leaving prison, and more than half were arrested by the end of the first year, meaning that the rate of recidivism was highest within the first year. These numbers do not reflect the individuals who get released and are murdered because of their relapse into criminal behavior or the individuals who simply have not gotten caught for their relapse into criminal behavior.

Recidivism is an issue attacking communities nationwide, because it promotes a certain type of behavior that sets everyone who possesses this sort of mentality to be subjected to adverse conditions. Households break, and children lack the proper guidance and structure necessary for positive development. Instead, the children become killers and gangbangers at an earlier age. It is difficult to be what you cannot see, and if you have a young mind that is highly impressionable, it is difficult not to get caught up in the lifestyle of criminal activity. It seems to be the most advantageous compared to the other options. When people get released from prison and still have the same mentality, or an even worse mentality than they did before they got incarcerated, that only produces others who adopt that same destructive mentality. It is critical for the person who is incarcerated to commit to a productive way of living because the success of the community depends on that individual's positive transformation.

If I am a twelve-year-old, my mind is still deciding which path I am committing to, and my environment—my household, the media, and my community—influences me. When looking at my household, I may see that it's all out of whack because my mother is trying to do everything on her own and my father is incarcerated. She is stressed because of her circumstances, causing her to make more bad decisions with bad men, and these men mean my development no good because their own development is no good. When I look at the media, I may see that the criminal lifestyle gets glamorized through movies and music. This makes it a bit more likely that I will adopt the same mentality—it seems as if you can survive the game, you will be able to live a life that is free and lovely. When I look at my community and see people committed to the criminal lifestyle making money hand over fist by committing to the game, it gets me closer to committing to this lifestyle myself. When I see people who are rapped about, admired, and glorified for their commitment to the game, and who finally get released from prison after serving a five- to ten-year prison sentence but still promote the same criminal behavior, this solidifies my commitment to the same game causing so much turmoil in society and my community. The person recidivating is ultimately the sole individual signing off on the destructive behavior.

A recidivist is sort of like the CEO of a going-backward lifestyle. The only thing worse than prison is death, and nobody but Jesus has come back from death, so the responsibility is huge for the returning citizen to describe prison exactly how it is. If that person returns to society with a positive outlook on life and refuses to go back to prison no matter the circumstances, this produces a truth that so many times gets overlooked, because it is not promoted. The question is not whether the people returning from prison are returning to lead. The question is which direction will they lead the people they have influence over?

Recidivism is a problem for the nation, and reducing the recidivism rate ultimately lowers the actual incarceration rate and increase public safety. More people will learn from the errors of the people returning from prison and choosing to lead a life that does not include prison.

Understanding the value of the returning citizen getting released from prison is reaching national attention and causing the federal government to fund programs under the Second Chance Act. These programs focus on reducing the recidivism rates, and they support organizations that help accomplish this mission. Taxpayers are growing weary of the same old philosophy of locking people up and releasing them from prison without the proper support to transition to a new, productive way of living. It costs taxpayers more money to incarcerate recidivists. There are programs under the Work Opportunity Tax Credit (WOTC) that encourage employers to hire returning citizens within the first year of release, giving the employer a tax credit of up to $2,400 for each qualifying employee. Unlike other programs that have a ceiling on the amount of tax credits that an employer can receive, this program has no cap on the number of people that can be hired. Businesses can receive the $2,400 tax credit for an unlimited number of individuals.

Community activists have gained ground with the "ban the box" campaign in which the employer cannot ask the question on an application, "Have you ever been convicted of a felony?" This question has been an issue with many individuals attempting to secure gainful employment after prison. They are not hired despite meeting the qualifications for the position. We have a nation focused on mass incarceration, whereas in the past, it was not as much of a topic as it is today.

The penal system in the state of Ohio is program-based so that individuals can get training in different fields to increase their likelihood of success. There are colleges, vocational training, and other programs inside the institution, which is designed to serve as a place of rehabilitation. Ohio is one of three states—along with California and North Dakota—that has *rehabilitation* in the actual name of the agency. The name of the agency is the Ohio Department of Rehabilitation and Correction, whereas most states just have *Department of Corrections* after the state's name. There is a lot in a name, and at 27.1 percent, Ohio currently has one of the lowest recidivism rates in the country. With that being said, Ohio is also at the top of the list for incarcerating individuals, which is in line with the nation in comparison to the rest of the world.

America makes up 5 percent of the world's population but makes up 25 percent of the world's incarcerated population. There are a recorded 2.2 million currently incarcerated in federal and state prisons across the nation. Nationally, the likelihood for an individual to recidivate is high, despite all the efforts to reduce the recidivism rate. Programs offered inside prisons are often not taken seriously, and individuals continue to program their minds in a way that will lead them back to prison, despite the fact that they do not like their situation. The hope of transitioning from their criminal mind-sets is nonexistent. This means that, despite all the programs and opportunities created to benefit these individuals during and after incarceration, hopes never get realized because the actual individuals do not see them as a greater opportunity than the one their criminal lifestyle presented to them. The fallout from this is families are destroyed and communities are ruined. The resources designed to help people transition from a criminal lifestyle to a legal, productive lifestyle are actually getting used to further support the criminal lifestyle. When people have not changed their thinking, and a program offers benefits such as clothing vouchers, driver's licenses, housing, and the like, those people will do what needs to be done to obtain those benefits then continue to live the criminal lifestyle lived before incarceration.

Having high-quality programming while an individual is incarcerated is the best approach to reducing the recidivism rate. High-quality programming means more than just presenting valuable information during the sessions; it also refers to the way that the sessions are implemented. When you have a case manager working for the state facilitating the program, it lowers the quality simply because actual participants are not convinced the information applies to them. Also, a lot of times, the case manager is disgruntled over the extra work, so the information does not get properly delivered. This approach gets a lot of inmates a certificate to show to their judge or parole board. While it does not promote a new way of thinking, it does sometimes result in their release, but they are unprepared despite attending all the required programming and having a certificate of attendance.

The best way to implement a program for this population is to have the program taught by an individual who has successfully made the transition, who has the same background, and who is able to vouch for the information because it assisted him or her personally. The program must be voluntary, because forcing someone to rehabilitate never truly works. If participation is mandatory, then that takes away from the quality of the program. The missing component that causes a lack of motivation is usually a lack of direction. When someone can see where he or she is headed, it breeds motivation all in itself. When you show a broken person somebody who was once broken but is now repaired, it creates a positive outlook in that person's mind. Prison is mostly mental, and you must be mentally strong to survive the experience.

Even with a program headed by an individual coming from the same experience as the population, there will still be sections of the prison population that will not attend and participate. Time is the most valuable asset known to mankind; it is the only thing you cannot get back. Once it's gone, it's gone. There will be people that will choose to waste time because they have not received the right information to do otherwise. If you waste your time during prison, then there is no chance for success after prison. Attending programs for a certificate, and not for a change in thinking and behavior, is a form of wasting time and it is expensive to waste your most valuable asset.

Being incarcerated is not comfortable to the spirit. I realized this at the beginning of my ten-year prison sentence. During my sentence, I saw men get released and return to prison within a matter of months. One common thing with all the people released and failing to stay out of prison was that they were all unproductive with their time concerning preparation for their release into society while incarcerated. Playing dominoes, cards, chess, and other board games all day is common. Gambling, using drugs, selling drugs, drinking alcohol, and hanging with individuals that promoted this lifestyle is also common.

I chose to do the opposite. I understood early on that this mind-set created failure. My idea of failure was getting released and having to come back to prison to do more time at a later date and watching my son come in and do time with me as well because of my reluctance to change. I was determined to make my walk match the walk I was going to conduct once I got released. I looked at the time in prison as practice, and the actual game was played on the other side of the fence. Your play in the game reflects the way you practice. So, I practiced on a new way of thinking that combated my current situation. Thinking controls behavior and I redesigned my behavior in a way that ensured I would not return to prison as an inmate. I always told people that my body was incarcerated, but my mind was working on freedom. Having the end in mind kept me with the needed direction and motivated throughout all the disappointments and setbacks. I maximized my time while I was incarcerated to evolve into a new individual, and it paid dividends for my future. The information in this book will assist you in doing the same and becoming a restored citizen.

2

Not in the Plans

PRISON DOES NOT just happen for most people, but it is a destination where you are committed and work over a period of time. I copped a plea to ten years for attempted murder, drug trafficking, possession of drugs, possession of firearms, and unlawful possession of a dangerous ordinance in February 1998. They did not have the wrong person. With my understanding of life at that time, I was definitely a threat to society and also myself.

While I was growing up, my household consisted of my father, grandmother, and brother. My mother got addicted to crack in the eighties and could not be there for me and my brother, so my father stepped up to the plate and raised us with my grandmother's help. Both my father and grandmother worked full-time jobs, so my brother and I had a lot of free time. We chose to hang in the streets, duplicating the street behavior we saw in movies, heard about in music, and saw firsthand from the dudes in the hood. It was just the four of us until my father met his soon-to-be wife, and we moved in together when I was in the seventh grade. My brother chose to stay with my grandmother, but I chose to go with my father and move to an apartment with his future wife, Donna, and her son, Shawka. Shawka and I were in the same grade in school and already friends, so to me this was going to be like a full-time sleepover. I was excited about the move.

I was that twelve-year-old child mentioned earlier working on a mentality that would bring the most success with the cards I had been dealt. I chose to begin selling marijuana and crack at thirteen years old. It seemed the most advantageous for me at that time. I was committed to the concept: if I could just work the streets for a period of time, then I would be able to transition into a legitimate successful business. I believed only the fools got caught, but I was going to be a different hustler. I was going to stay on my toes at all times and stack my money. I would not speak during drug sales for fear of a wiretap. I would keep my drugs in my underwear. I would only deal with a selected few, and I would punish anyone who went against my millionaire mission and me.

I had it all planned until, unfortunately, that plan went astray. I had to make a move on one of my close friends after he stole $1,000 in crack. It was not the amount as much as it was the principle that hurt the most. The hurt drove me to the point of feeling as though I had to murder him. There was no way I could continue selling drugs and make a profit if people knew I let somebody stealing from me slide. I was already on bond after getting pulled over on a traffic stop. The police had searched my vehicle and discovered about a half ounce of individually bagged crack, about a thousand dollars in cash, a sawed-off .410-gauge shotgun, and a stolen brand-new 9 millimeter with the serial number scratched off in my trunk. I obtained a good lawyer and was confident in my chances of beating the case. Why I was confident is a mystery to me. Maybe it was all the weed I smoked producing this confidence.

With all of that going on in my mind, a simple fight didn't suffice for the trespass my good friend had committed. I was dedicated to this street way of living, and I was willing to die, or commit murder if need be, to maintain the lifestyle. This mentality was developed from the lies I had been told about the way to live. Those were the rules that one must follow to be successful on the streets. If you had money, then you were successful. Money equaled freedom. It did not matter how it was gotten. I was convinced and committed to the concept.

I recall my heart was black during my time navigating through the streets. It was necessary for operating in that game. I sold dope to mothers in front of their children. I sold dope to pregnant women. I took from the perceived weak and pistol-whipped addicts who did not have the money they owed me. Through it all, I had a vision that I would be able to come out of this game and be a benefit to the people I was connected to in my circle. Ultimately, I wanted to benefit to my newborn son and provide the best for him. I wanted to make sure he grew up differently than I did.

Instead of all the luxuries I had envisioned, I received a ten-year sentence in a place that seemed to be right next door to hell. I was scheduled to spend all my twenties inside this place. My son would be ten years old by the time I was released. That's when reality set in, and I began to redesign myself. I was determined to become an individual who did not have another incarceration on my horizon.

Change first starts from within. It starts within yourself, and it starts within your current situation. The change in my mind occurred when I was at the beginning of my prison term, and it's what led me to be successful behind bars and later become successful upon release. I learned that there is a process to change, and just because you make the decision to change in your mind, this does not mean that all your actions will reflect that change.

Living like I had, for so many years, made it challenging to abandon that way of thinking completely. I struggled from time to time with making the transition into a new, improved individual, one who managed life differently. When someone from your neighborhood expects to see this wild, live-wire individual, but they get an individual who is evolving into somebody different instead, it is tempting to revert back into the individual they had grown to love and respect. During these lapses, I found myself slipping into the darkness and backsliding to some of those old habits I was convinced would not get me anything that I desired—but this is the struggle. It's all in the mind.

On occasion, I found myself around these individuals from my same city, and they always had weed. Being around them as much as I was broke through the theory of doing everything differently to get different results. While I was in prison, I hit the weed a few times just to experience the feeling I'd had back on the streets. I recall going two years without smoking weed and I took a couple of puffs of a pin joint. I was high as a kite. I could not stop laughing. It felt as if I was thirteen again, when I first started smoking weed with my brother. Although it was fun at the time, what drove me back to reality was when inside sources told us that random urine tests were going to be conducted after the weekend was over. I could not afford to get caught with weed in my system, get sent to segregation, and not be able to see my son for the "My Child and I Day" festival coming up. He really enjoyed himself at the bi-annual event, and I did not want to take that away from him just because I wanted to have fun smoking weed. I drank gallons and gallons of water and drank warm water right before the test. By the grace of God, I passed the drug test.

The struggle is always doing what you know is right and what is going to put you in the best situation versus doing what you're accustomed to doing for years. Change is a process that takes time and commitment. If you erase either of those two, change will not happen. That's why it does not work when people are released from prison, because they erased one of the mandatory ingredients from the recipe for change to occur: time.

I remember I used to run toward the drama. Now, I had to run away from the drama. I used to respect only a certain type of individual. Now, I had to respect everyone. I was determined to walk differently, talk differently, and act differently to get different results.

I observed the mentalities of those who failed upon their release because there was nobody to study who had succeeded after prison. It seemed that if you became successful after prison, you were encouraged to keep a lid on your past. If you did not, there were people who would want to take your success away. I discovered that getting into productive activities was critical, but it had to be productive. It was not productive if learning was not taking place. People enrolled in the same programs I was had different levels of success because their goals were different. I focused on becoming a better individual to live life in a more desirable place, whereas others' goals were just to burn time, get some food at the completion of the program for graduation, or present a case that they were different people and deserved a second chance to a decision maker for early release. They wanted to look like a different person but think the same. These individuals got the opportunity to go home through early release or parole only to return back to prison within the first year. A few individuals were even murdered within the first year of their releases.

I studied scripture and surrounded myself with people just as dissatisfied as me in a place such as this. This gave me the most support to begin combatting the old way of thinking that had gotten me by for so many years.

I remember being very aggressive in my vision of becoming rich by selling drugs, and that was what had gotten me ten years in prison. I had to apply that same level of aggression into my rehabilitation to become a new and improved individual. My thoughts about prison started changing my thoughts about the streets. I looked at prison as a simulator to death and also a simulator to hell. It was not actually death or hell, but I felt it was close.

If you look at what takes place before a person dies, it's similar to prison. When you die, you cannot take any possessions you obtained with you. When you are in prison, you cannot take any of your possessions with you when you go through processing. When you die, you have to separate from the people you love. When you go to prison, you cannot take the people you love with you. When you are in hell, I envisioned it as torture. I believe a part of that torture is in knowing what's coming every day, and there are no surprises in life. In prison, you know you are going to eat at the same time every day. You are going to see the same people every day. You know that when the store day runs, you are going to get the same five cans of tuna, twenty packages of Ramen Noodles, three cans of Jack Mack, two bags of chips, three jugs of Kool-Aid, and one jar of coffee. Your overall structure is going to be basically the same from day to day. Even the new people who come are not new most of the time. They have recidivated and are coming back to the same institution to do more time. Even if they have not been incarcerated before, they are usually the son or relative of an individual who has been incarcerated, and they look and act just like the individual that you knew.

Looking at prison as being close to death and being right next door to hell drove my desire to be successful. I did not want my son experiencing penitentiary time. I was determined to overcome this experience and be able to give my son an honest summary of what the streets and penitentiary life was about, the summary that I hadn't received at the age of twelve when I'd been deciding what type of life I was going to lead. I had been influenced by people coming home saying that prison was a piece of cake, and they had done the time standing on their heads.

What I have figured out is that nobody really feels like that. Everybody wants to go home, nobody is comfortable, and everybody misses their relationships that they had while free. The fear of change is what keeps people sticking to the same mentality and ultimately sticking to a destructive path. I was on the streets to be in a position to call the shots and live life to the fullest, because I believed it was possible.

The person incarcerated is vitally critical to the movement of changing the community and changing the nation. The best chance a twelve-year-old contemplating getting involved in the streets and engaging in a criminal lifestyle has is to be given the information by the person returning from prison. You cannot return from actual death or hell to tell people the life they are living, or thinking about living, is one that will bring about this type of discomfort. If that person comes home and says the experience is near death and hell's neighbor and that they will never put themselves in a position to go back to prison because nothing is worth that price or sacrifice, then that confused twelve-year-old has better information and the ability to make an informed decision. When that individual also holds a certain level of respect in the neighborhood, this strategy will be highly effective. A person who can say that there is nothing in the world worth going to prison for is powerful.

I was a person that was "street" to the core, and I believed it to the core. I was afraid of neither death nor penitentiary. People did not think anything could change me from that mentality. This made my change valuable to the community because of the influence I already possessed. To see me change encouraged people to emulate my change.

I took this drive, and I completed my ten years inside a correctional facility with no Rules Infractions Board (RIB) convictions. The RIB enforced rules that were broken with a stay in segregation. These rules also went on your record, and kept you from participating in certain programs. I was able to graduate college with a 3.83 GPA and also graduate from administrative office technology in vocational training. I was determined to pounce on anything that had value to counter the fact that I was sitting in a prison adding value to others' lives by providing them with a salary and employment because of the errors in my thinking. I was convinced the only way I was going to be able to survive all the challenges that so many people before me had faced and failed was to be able to face and conquer the challenges while incarcerated. To be successful once you get released, you have to live in prison without bars.

3

Redesign Yourself

PRISON WITHOUT BARS backs the theory that in order to become successful once you leave the penitentiary, you must first become successful while you are still incarcerated. If you cannot make the proper decisions while incarcerated, you will not be able to make them once released. It's almost like Tim Tebow, when he played quarterback for the Denver Broncos. The coaches were unimpressed with his practicing, but people tried to vie for his ability due to what he had done in college and say he was a game-day player, not a practice player. Well, when game time arrived, the results were not much different. He received the lowest quarterback rating the game had seen in years. If you practice terribly, you play terribly. If you do time in an unproductive way, then that is the same way you will do your time when you get released, and you are more likely to recidivate. If you cannot stay out of segregation, then you will not be able to stay out of the back of a police car once you get released. I saw it happen all too many times throughout my ten-year prison sentence. You could tell who was going to come back to prison. You have to become a new individual and redesign yourself in order to accomplish success while in prison. Success in prison gives you the ability to maintain your own structures once the structure of prison is gone. You begin transitioning back into the community the day you get incarcerated, not once your release date arrives. If you wait until then, it is too late, and you will recidivate.

In *Prison without Bars*, we cover the six major areas you have to pay attention to in order to redesign yourself. These steps will help you become an individual who has gathered all the scattered pieces from his or her broken past back together. You can form a picture that satisfies you, and recidivism will not be included inside that picture.

The first area of focus to become successful inside the penitentiary is having a one-on-one conversation with yourself to figure out what your idea of success is. This is the most important aspect of beginning the change needed to transition back into society. The perception most people get wrong with incarcerated individuals is that, because they commit crimes, they do not have the desire to be successful and they are okay with being incarcerated. This is the most preposterous assumption, and I find myself always correcting people. One of the major reasons people return to prison is because they did not do a one-on-one intervention with themselves to figure out what success actually means to them.

The next area of focus for a successful transition into this new way of living is usually the first thing you hear about when people find themselves in situations like these: submitting to a higher power. Religion gives you the hope needed to combat all the negative thoughts that you will receive in this situation.

The next area of focus is changing the way you speak. Your language has a lot to do with how you behave and what you attract. Then, you must focus on choosing the right individuals to interact with on a daily basis. You are who you are around.

Another area to focus on is making decisions in a different way that makes sense for you.

One of the most important areas to focus on is understanding time is valuable. You must learn to utilize it in productive ways. The biggest obstacle you will face accomplishing this gigantic goal is ultimately yourself. This is the main reason people do not lead a life that fits them. They, instead, live a life that fits the eyes and thoughts of other people. People choose not to change because they fear what their peers will think of them if they stop putting themselves in the same risky situations. Being alone is the most challenging state to embrace. Many people do not even think it is possible to change. Often, you have to walk this walk with many people you did not grow up with. People will stay the same for fear of the unknown, even if the known is possibly a disaster. They will take the possible disaster versus the unknown.

Another obstacle is not having a mentor to help you along with this process. If you're in a situation where everybody is trying to figure out how to get the best out of life, sometimes this situation will offer few mentors to guide you through the process. This book serves as a mentor. Access to the thoughts of someone who has successfully transitioned into society and redesigned himself is huge. After being released for eight years, I can honestly say that I have not been around, or even seen, any pistols or any crack since before I was incarcerated. What I did while incarcerated prepared me to accomplish that gigantic task.

The last obstacle is not being committed enough because your "why" is not great enough to commit to this change. As with anything in life, your commitment will determine your success.

The best way to overcome the obstacles to living the life you want is understanding that, at the end of the day, no one will hurt like the actual person being inflicted with the pain. I always tell people that I have the right to change in a way that fits me.

I realized that nobody was included in my identification badge but me. While you're incarcerated, letters from the people you are living to impress are few and far between—if you receive any letters at all. Nobody is vying to complete some of your prison term for you. No one is even checking up on your children or family members while you are gone. Their lives go on, and for you to stay committed to something that is not committed to you just does not make sense. Having the courage to say you are going to take your better life, no matter what the cost, is the way you overcome the obstacles.

I was once told that if you do not have a seat at the table, then more than likely, it's because you are on the menu. "Sitting at the table" simply means you are benefiting from a particular situation rather than existing for the sole purpose of benefiting someone else. It's okay to benefit someone else as long as you receive benefits as well. Information influences thinking, and thinking controls behavior.

Thinking about prison in a whole new light will combat the main obstacle to living in prison without bars. The biggest barrier to overcoming prison is overcoming you, and doing what is necessary to change.

4

Identify Success

BEFORE YOU CAN accomplish any goal in life, the first step is recognizing what the actual goal is. So many people do not give this the proper attention. They lack a true direction and become the people helping the accomplishment of other people's goals. If you are not utilizing yourself in the correct way, then people will utilize you in the correct way for their own purposes. Everybody is used while on this earth, but it is when we are misused that people are left in undesirable situations. Prison is filled with individuals who do not have proper direction, and therefore, a direction is manufactured for them to fulfill somebody else's mission. People who have proper direction do not put themselves in a situation such as prison.

I discussed earlier that prison is a place that is similar to death or close to hell. Anybody with direction will not let prison be an option. I believe this goes back to our ideology of success. When our ideology of success is formed from the media and entertainment, we struggle with true direction. This is because we do not have a true definition of ourselves. We define ourselves by how our environment defines us. When I was on the streets, if you were broke, then you were at the bottom of the barrel. Successful people had money, and unsuccessful people did not have money. Although money is a part of success, what I found out is that this is not the entirety of the ingredients making up my idea of success. It takes more than money to be successful, in my eyes.

PRISON WITHOUT BARS

Determining what makes your life enjoyable is the question that you must answer before you can begin to evolve into the individual that fits your heart.

When I was in prison and realized I had to do the next ten years of my life in a correctional facility, I came to the conclusion that this was not my idea of success. I began to look at the life I had led up until that point. I asked myself how much joy I had experienced. I made a decent amount of money during my stint selling drugs from thirteen to nineteen years old, but I recalled I was never really comfortable. The game presented different losses, and it was like a roller coaster. I might have to run from the police and throw my product, or I might buy some bad product that presented me with a loss. I feared drug raids for secret indictments, because I did not know if I was on the list. I was especially afraid when they were arresting a lot of people that were very close to me. I could not trust people in general because of the jealousy the street element produces. I fell out with my family because of my dedication to getting money. I was convinced if I got money, I would be successful. I thought money put me in a position to call the shots. Money gave me freedom. Money filled all the potholes in my life.

When you grow up in an environment with limited money, it is perceived that the main reason for the ills of life revolves around money. I would say that 80 percent of crimes have a great deal to do with money: trying to rob, steal, sell drugs, or even do drugs in an attempt to escape the depression caused by the lack of money. Money is an issue.

The foundation of my change came in understanding what success meant to me. I realized money and materialistic items alone were not enough for me to enjoy life. I was in this place, and even if I had millions of dollars, I still would not be content. I wanted the ability to be able to see my son grow. I wanted to be around people that I knew cared about me and involved in genuine relationships. I wanted to change my environment in the same day. I wanted to travel. I wanted to watch a Cavs game. I wanted to watch the Browns play. I wanted to eat gelatin with fruit in it when I wanted. I wanted some soft things in my life versus everything hard, which surrounded me in prison. The toilet paper was hard. The cots were hard and small with no room to roll over, and all I could do was flip over. The water coming out of the shower head was hard. And most of all, the legs that filled the dorms and cellblocks were hard. Being counted six times a day, like cattle, rubbed me the wrong way as well. My name was reduced to a six-digit number, and living out of a two-by-four-foot locker box was not my idea of success either. I was a legal slave, not because I was forced to be one, but because the law of the land said that I was one, officially.

The Thirteenth Amendment reads: "Neither slavery nor involuntary servitude, except as punishment for a crime whereof the party shall have been duly convicted, shall exist in the United States, or any other place subject to their jurisdiction." The only way that anyone can be a slave in the United States of America now is to be convicted of a crime, and it serves as punishment! This is why people working in the furniture factory can get paid twenty-two cents an hour for producing furniture for businesses that make millions of dollars in revenue a year.

Prison is a business, and I was the product. This was a part of the game that I did not sign up for at all. I was only supposed to get the money and all the luxuries it had to offer, but instead, I received a ten-year sentence. All these wants I had weren't met with me being in prison. When I was on the streets, the main goal was not to be hustled and not be treated as a sucker. I felt like a sucker because the money I hustled for was confiscated due to being drug money. The cars I bought were considered purchased with drug money and confiscated. The only thing not considered drug money and not questioned was the money that I took to my attorney. If the drug money was bad and needed to be confiscated, then how an attorney could be permitted to accept this tainted drug money?

These thoughts rained through my mind and made me more determined and dedicated to change so I would not be in a position where my foolishness and suffering paid someone else's salary. I viewed the attorney as being a part of a system where people on the other side of it never really truly won. I did not like putting my life in the hands of others.

My change was driven by my true desire not to be on the short end of the stick. I knew that if I did not figure this prison life out in a way that greatly increased my likelihood of being successful once I got released, then it was highly likely my son would grow up to do the same things. I was creating my "why." If you do not have a big enough "why," then evolving into an individual who will be successful once released is not likely. Everything that I wanted to accomplish in life did not equal penitentiary. Knowing your definition of success is the beginning of evolving into a new individual. Knowing is half the battle.

Sometimes people find it difficult to figure out what their idea of success is. When that occurs, do not be discouraged. Instead, build it from the back end to figure your idea of success. What that means is figuring out places you do not want to be. Think of situations you have been in and do not want to revisit. Think of things you have seen happen to others that you would not want happening to you. This is a great start to achieving what you want your life to look like. You base it off what you definitely do *not* want it to look like. The key to living in prison without bars is living a life that suits you.

Understanding this allowed me to focus on my rehabilitation and begin taking a stand against the characteristics that backed the type of living contradictory to my vision of success. I refused to be a sucker, so I decided to make the most of my time in prison by preparing for the future. I treated this situation like college and improved every part of my game physically, spiritually, and mentally. I just knew that my idea of success was not prison, that I had the power to change it, and that I would succeed.

Change first starts within yourself and then extends to your current situation. My change began once I realized that my current situation was not success. A popular saying in the penitentiary is when you are tired of being sick and tired, that's when true change begins. Something has to happen when you do not have the energy to continue the race the way that you are running it. Some sort of change occurs. Whether you sit down and catch your breath, or you pass out, something changes about your race. When you can honestly say you are tired of living life a certain way, the evolution begins at that point. I found out that when people look for the environment to change before they choose to change then that change never happens, because the environment never changes. Once you change, the environment has no choice but to fall in line.

I did not care a thing about the changing of laws, lack of job opportunities, cases where people had failed, or any other barrier that could possibly be a threat to my change for the better. I made the decision that this was not going to be my life anymore, and I was not waiting on everything to fall into place in order to retire from this misery. I did not wait for everything to fall into place to get money when I was dealing drugs. I went out there, and I took it! I did not get distracted when it was below-zero weather and my feet and my hands were frozen. I stayed on the block until I sold out. I applied this same mentality to my pursuit of a better life, so I could be the man I desired to be. I wanted to be the father I needed to be so my child could experience the things in life that I desired for him.

People who are incarcerated do not face the issue of commitment but *what* they are committed to. People will put their lives on the line for their gang, their money, their jewelry, and their reputations. I believe that is due to those twelve-year-olds developed to value the things that are not worth much, so in turn, they live a life that is below value for them. Once these individuals get the right information and recommitted to a life that makes sense, the sky is the limit. I was committed to my old life. I decided to commit to my new life—a life without bars.

5

Higher Power

"IF YOU DO not find something to stand for, then you will fall for anything." An older individual spoke these words during his twenty-sixth year of incarceration. He did not have any proof of whether his ideology was true or not because he had not been able to test that theory in his community, but I took it as true. That is a profound phrase that a lot of individuals who are incarcerated throw around lightly, but it is not to be taken lightly. Now, after being released from prison for more than eight years, I can honestly say this is a true phrase. Your success depends on how you do your time. How you do your time stems from what you choose to stand for or believe in.

Once I came to the conclusion that my old lifestyle was not profitable, I decided to put my disdain for my current situation to use. I decided that I did not want to be labeled a sucker or somebody else's bridge to his or her own personal success while I got walked on and worn down. I was adamant about utilizing my time to become a new and improved individual who reached all-time heights.

The first thing I chose to do was acquaint myself with scripture. The only way I was going to be able to survive and live a life worth living was by getting new information to influence my thinking. During my childhood, I never went to church because my father and grandmother did not go, and they did not require it of my brother and me. My other grandmother, from the South, went to church, but the way we got out of it was by simply saying that we did not have anything to wear. It worked every time, and we grew up not knowing anything about the Bible or Christianity.

Grandma Lynn introduced me to the scriptures after I got pulled over, and the police found the guns, drugs, and money in my trunk, and I had to fight the case from the streets once I made bail. I was staying with Grandma Lynn at the time, and I recall before going to my pretrial, she had me sit in a tub filled with some sort of spices and oils and read the book of Psalms. I was desperate, so I was willing to try anything. If this got me probation for my cases, I was willing to give it an honest shot. I had read some scripture that had caught my attention but disregarded it because, although I was on bail, I was still heavy in the street lifestyle. I probably turned up another notch after my case, because I felt I had to do twice as much with the case hanging over my head. It was not enough for me to change my thinking at the time, but it was a seed that got planted that I later explored.

So, once I got to prison and wanted to redesign myself, I really heard what the Word was saying, because I was sincerely seeking to become a better person. I saw a lot of people going that route, which I think is a natural reaction when faced with these types of circumstances. What I saw, though, was people attempting to use religion in the same manner that I had been—not serious and really trying to find a new way of thinking but trying to get the hookup from God so they could continue to do what they were doing. I was going through the motions, because that was what Grandma Lynn said I should do to get me out of the jam I was in. I noticed the people I was incarcerated with doing the same thing. It is always easy to identify a mentality in others that you once possessed.

I started going to Bible study and reading the Bible from Genesis to Revelation. I did not go to church because I did not want to be in the midst of the singing. I just wanted to study the Word so I could become wise. I was seeking, and that meant all the difference in the world. I was convinced that my way was not working, and I was open to any suggestions to help me be where I wanted to be in life. I chose to read scripture and apply it to my life.

Having faith in a higher power is vital to living in prison without bars. It helps you have faith that your current situation, which is hell, is not final. Faith is what got me through my prison term with a sane mind. The more I read the Bible, the more faith I had in God and the good that he had in store for me. I understood that anything that I went through would not be more than I could bear. I could overcome all things if I only possessed a faith in God as big as a grain of mustard seed. After understanding that I did not want my life to look like it did anymore, my faith pushed me to evolve into an individual forever combatting this sort of situation. I went from being disgusted with my situation to doing something about being disgusted. I was evolving into something great, and it felt promising.

The more I read the bible, the more confidence I had, which was something I had not experienced before. The verse "greater is he that is in me than he that is the world" just gave me a certain type of confidence needed in prison. When I was on the streets, everything I thought about myself was based on the way other people thought about me. Now, I was focused on the way God thought about me. I believed he was in control, and my actions supported that belief. One thing I knew was that people are never satisfied, so why live life according to them? At the end, they can only offer you so much.

Listening to what everybody else thinks about you in a situation when you are experiencing clear failure is detrimental to your evolution. Everything with prison is mental, and getting your definition of yourself from other people will have your mind in a defeated state. There will be correctional officers who treat you as if you are less than a man. The system of prison in itself is designed to make you feel demeaned and worthless. So many people buy into this way of thinking, and this is what they act out in the long run. This becomes reality for them for decades to come. Even family members and friends express their disappointment in your failures. There is no way to combat that but through some form of religion. Religion conditions your mind to understand that you are still very valuable, even though everybody around you suggests otherwise. You see broken people in prison without the support to be repaired because they look for support in places that it will not come from, so they suffer.

I started to change, and people saw it. I began with my language because the Word said that the tongue is the smallest muscle in the body, but it's the hardest to control, and yet it defiles the whole body. I ceased the talking littered with curse words and chose different words to replace those words. I used words such as *stuff* instead of *shit*. I used *dang* instead of *damn*. I used *brotha* instead of *nigga*. I did not want to talk like a person that has prison in his future. I trained my mind to talk like I would in front of Grandma and just replaced the concept of my grandma with God to keep myself disciplined in my language. If I had enough respect for Grandma not to curse and talk recklessly in front of her, then I could have the same respect for God. The Word indicates that if you talk differently, you act differently. I got my wisdom from the ultimate source controlling the universe. Spirituality changes your outlook on life. It transforms your mind if you take it seriously.

I do not promote one religion over the other. I believe that if you follow the principles in the religions, then you will be productive in your everyday living. It's when people try to distort the scriptures to fit their own ideologies that there is conflict. Believing in a higher power besides yourself and people on this earth is critical to becoming successful in prison and, ultimately, outside of prison. It gives you the ability to walk with a power that cannot be denied. It does not say that challenging things will not happen to you, but it provides a different way to look at the things that happen to you due to your faith in your higher power. It's how I battled getting denied for judicial release four times, not getting visits from my son's mother, not being able to get through to people on the outside via phone, missing my son, dealing with staff who looked at me as something less than a human being, and having to complete an entire decade in a correctional facility, just to name a few.

The emotions involved while incarcerated can be damaging if not managed properly. I saw people attempting to manage these emotions with their own understanding, and it never worked. Looking at this situation without a spiritual lens causes a depressing situation, and your actions correspond with your state of mind. Prison challenges your sanity in a way that, if you survive it, you will possess a strength that will get you through the most extreme challenges life has to offer. You will understand through experience, if it is put on your plate, then you can handle it. God will not allow you to go through anything that will overcome you and that you cannot handle. Having the ability to handle things when it is going great does not take that much effort. The true effort is handling things in a respectable manner when it is not going so great. Faith in God gives you the ability to accomplish that.

6

Who They Are Is Who You Are

"*H*E WHO WALKS with wise men shall become wise but he who walks with fools will be devoured" (Proverbs 13:20). This scripture has resonated with me ever since the first time I read these profound words. Different quotes speaking about this scripture have been in society for generations. "Watch the company you keep" and "birds of a feather flock together" are two of the most common that I recall hearing during my childhood.

The people you are around on a daily basis and who dominate the majority of your time will determine where you are going and who you are going to be in life. We have on average five people who we are around the most in our lives that influences our character. Show me who your friends are, and I will show you who you are.

I remember, in the streets, different groups of characters all did basically the same things. The people robbing others were in a particular group, and they all looked for opportunities to steal. The people selling drugs hung around each other, and they always looked for the best dope and lowest prices. The people wanting to just get high also hung around together, and they sought out for the best deals for their money to get high. Somebody who was broke and did not have money was not going to be able to hang around the people that had money. That approach to the topic was totally different, which meant the only way the relationship worked was if one abandoned his or her philosophy and adopted the other person's philosophy.

Somebody might never have heard you speak one word, but if they see you around a bunch of people with questionable morals on a continuous basis, they assume you have those same questionable morals, and they separate themselves from you. You lose opportunities based on the people that you have chosen to hang around. With that being said, you could gain opportunities based on the people that you are associated with as well.

People went home and were murdered, not because of an act they committed but because they were in the wrong place at the wrong time with the wrong person. People have recidivated in a matter of months, because they went home and got involved with the same groups and got caught up in racketeering charges, because they were in all the camera shots during the investigation. Saying they were not involved in selling drugs was not enough to keep them out of prison. Who you are around is detrimental to your success.

Going through a criminal case will get you in the state of mind that you do not have that many people pushing for you when you are at the bottom. Being introduced to prison made me focus on myself more than anything. I realized that if I did not take care of myself, then the next person was not going to take care of me. I vowed I would not leave my success or failures in another person's hands. I was going to make decisions according to my own growth and advancement. Those who really cared about me would applaud those decisions. Those who did not really care about me would not.

When you're incarcerated, you hear stories of life going on without you. Your friends will scream, "Free so-and-so," but that is as far as it goes. The parties will continue, the game will continue, whether you are there or not. You rarely see people get support from the people they would be attempting to impress if they were free. The support often comes from your parents and, maybe, your significant other. I have always been a man who, once something makes sense to me, can devote myself to it wholeheartedly. It made sense to dedicate myself to my development.

I recall being thirteen and dumbing myself down to fit in with the crowd. I could have gotten merit and honor roll in school, but it seemed a lot cooler to get bad grades then good grades. Some of my friends really struggled and could not do better without the proper tutoring, but that was not the case for me. I did not want them to make fun of me, so I chose to underperform to make them feel comfortable. That was an error in my thinking. Excelling would have only opened doors for others while my underperforming only kept the doors closed for those who could have used it open. Fitting in with the crowd is hard work, and it is a disservice to you.

Marion Correctional Institution had a prison population of roughly about 2,400 inmates when I was incarcerated. Twenty-four hundred people from different cities and backgrounds I had to study and learn in order for me to be successful in the penitentiary. Who to associate with and who not to associate with can be critical, not only in prison but throughout life in general. Growing up on the streets gave me a head start on making the correct associations. Failure is the tuition to success, and I had failed in choosing the right associates in the past. This failure brought me many losses, but I was able to learn from those losses, so actually, it was a gain. I learned to read people a lot better. The streets teach you to do that through experience. Being thirteen and involved in a game where I had to deal with grown men made me grow up quickly as far as reading people was concerned.

I studied people and always looked at them with a keen eye and left no room for the garbage. I presented myself as an individual not looking for friends or looking to join any crews for protection. I was not looking to connect with new people. I was looking to do my time and get out of that place and be the person who never went back there again. I had a few people I knew from the streets in my dorm, and I spoke with them, but I wasn't clingy. I did not know what they had been doing before I had arrived at the institution. I wanted any problems put on my plate to be problems that I created myself, not somebody else's. There were people I grew up with that I had to separate from, because the way they were living was suspect, and I did not want to be associated with that type of living. They could have been robbing people or even engaging in homosexual activity. Whatever the case, I did not want to be labeled and guilty by association. I did not care if people went home and said that I did not "kick it" with them. I was focused on my own development. My faith in God really did assist me with my walk, because I felt as though I did not need anyone but God, and that gave off a powerful aura that other people respected. I chose people to associate with that fit my criteria for my growth. Coming from the same hood was not enough to make the cut. Being able to go to the commissary every week was not enough to make the cut. You had to be an individual that assisted me in my growth. You had to be at a place I was aiming to get to mentally, or you had to be going to the same place I wanted to be mentally. In this environment, you saw people hanging with people because of their commissary or because they came from the same neighborhood. People became Muslims because they felt like that Islamic faith offered the most protection when they were in prison due to their strength in numbers. In turn, they did not seek the religion to change the way that they were thinking but for the protection they felt they needed from the many Muslims flooding the penitentiary.

It did not take me long to figure out who was who in this environment. You had the type that put their "religion face" on as a distraction of who they really were. It was a game to them, and the motive was not to get closer to God but rather to get closer to your commissary or even closer to you sexually. They quoted all the scriptures and always talked about God, but the fruits that grew from their tree were rotten. I made it my business to stay away from such individuals. I learned from them from afar, and they helped me in my walk toward becoming a better person. I did not want to look like a person who was into the Bible with my talk but one whose actions said something else. I made it a point to be as real as possible with my devotion to the Word to avoid looking like a hypocrite.

The next character is the person who tries too hard to be noticed and involved with other people. This is usually due to being scared or just insecure, and it shows. This character is always attempting to start a conversation and looking for a new friend. This is the individual who will give his commissary in order to make some friends because he does not want to be alone, but he still ends up alone when he does not have anything to give. That does not take long when you are feeding a group of individuals on a daily basis.

I rarely took part in the group breaks, which is Ramen Noodles, some sort of meat, mayo, cheese, and chips all mixed together. I did not want to use all my mayonnaise or cheese in a couple of breaks. It would feed ten people, but then I wouldn't have that condiment later in the week. It made more sense for me to be as independent as possible, and I ate a soup and a half along with tuna, a squirt of mayonnaise, and cheese once a day. My cheese and mayonnaise, which is the most expensive, lasted a couple of weeks that way. I made sure I went to the chow hall for lunch and dinner to preserve my commissary. My commissary lasted the entire week, so I did not have to go borrow from somebody else.

Then you have to watch out for the one who burned all his bridges with his family, and he gets nothing sent in from the outside. He looks for those who are weak and pounces on them to survive the penitentiary. He will be the friendliest because he has nothing in his own mind, and he is doing what needs to be done to be the main guy on the receiving end of commissary. This same character also uses the fear approach to get what he wants. He knows who is afraid, and he extorts that individual. I stayed away from this type as well. If they burned their bridges with the people that loved them on the streets, then there was a good chance that they'd burn the bridges connected to me if given the chance. It was only a matter of time before they picked the wrong person and got hurt or even killed. The people who are scandalous on the streets are still scandalous in prison.

I made it my business to surround myself with good-hearted individuals wanting to expand their knowledge. There is always a duality going on when you are trying to make this change between the old you and the new you. When you're an outlaw for so long, it is a major challenge to transition into the mind-set of a civilian, especially when you have so many people around you promoting the outlaw mentality. This is the ultimate challenge in becoming free behind bars—detaching from the people you recognize the most and attaching instead to the unfamiliar. If you are around the outlaw mentality and you are trying to transition from that mentality, it will be next to impossible to make that transition for the simple fact that those individuals around you will always bring the outlaw mentality out of you.

I knew the benefits that outlaw mentality provided. One of those benefits was my current situation. I had to change my circle if I was going to accomplish changing my mentality.

7

Decisions Need to Be Made

THE CHOICES THAT we make determine the destination of our lives. We have been given freedom of choice, and this freedom is what keeps us incarcerated mentally and physically. Wherever you are in life, you made some sort of decision to end up in that position. Realizing this did not make me feel depressed, but optimistic. If I made the choice to be in my current environment, then I could also make the choice to not be in prison after I completed my prison term.

I remember coming to grips with the fact that it was not the police, it was not the system; it was not my family or friends that got me here. It was my decisions that got me here. Once I realized that, a lot of anger released. Quite frankly, people can only be angry with themselves for a period of time. I had to go about making my decisions in a different manner—a manner that was carefully analyzed and would put me in premier situations.

When I was selling dope, I recall making decisions based on the benefits I received. I only saw the large amounts of cash and the freedom that drugs brought to my life. I did not take time to evaluate the negative consequences thoroughly; therefore, I made poor choices. Gathering an understanding of what the picture is revealing with only a sliver of details from the actual image is not the foundation for making good decisions. If I had sincerely calculated that prison or death was highly likely, I would have made a different choice.

What good does it do if I make money only to get it confiscated? This was one of several questions I asked myself. Was shaving years off my life worth getting my money? If I hustled for my family, would they benefit more if I was there, or would they benefit more if I got a whole bunch of money but my presence was absent? I never wanted to lose in anything I was involved with, and the streets were no different.

I began to put all my decisions under scrutiny. These were the decisions that had put me in a place I did not want to be. I had to evaluate those decisions and see the error in my thinking in order to place myself in better situations.

Reflecting on all my decisions was what made me humble. I knew I had made some terrible decisions, and they were made while I was only looking at part of the picture. I could not be angry with anybody because I made the decisions. No one made them for me. There were people who glorified my case because I shot my friend at point-blank range in the head over his betrayal, for stealing a sack of crack. I did not back this decision, and I expressed my regret when people tried to glorify this act.

I recall that night, when I had him in the car, and I took him to the back roads. I was not comfortable with doing it then. I just felt as though I had no choice once I pulled the pistol out and put it to his head. I had committed, and in my mind, I could not turn back. I had thought about it for months, and when the time came to make my move, it was nothing like I thought it was going to be. I felt remorse, and I did not feel good about killing my friend. I had a reputation to uphold, so I pulled the trigger. I tried to justify it at the time by saying he was a thief and he got what he deserved, but in reality, a human life—especially the life of a friend I had known my whole life—was not worth materialistic items.

Understanding the pain I had caused due to my poor decision made me more analytical with my decisions. I was determined to make decisions by taking all the information into account first. If I did not have a sufficient amount of information, then my decision was to not make a decision.

I started replacing my bad decisions with good decisions by being conscious of what I was doing.

Making the decision to change the way I lived life was the first good decision I made. I have seen people not satisfied with the results they have gotten, yet they continue to do the same exact thing expecting to get a different result. This is despite the fact that they have not seen anyone before them be able to accomplish this feat.

Analyzing my true definition of success versus what I had been told was my second good decision. I realized that what I was chasing was missing a lot of the elements that were the most important to me. If relationships were important, then I had to nurture them rather than treating them as though they were expendable. I made sure when I got through to my family on the phone, they knew I valued them, despite my past actions, and I was thankful for them being in my life. I wanted to be a positive individual in order to get positive results. I was determined to extend the same level of realness to everybody instead of only toward the people I felt were worthy.

Everything revolved around me in my decision-making process. Now, some people will hear that and say I was selfish, but this is what you must do to be successful and a benefit to everyone around you. I understood that I was the one accountable for the decisions I made, so it was a must that I be okay with the decision 100 percent. It is a red flag when someone tells me they are doing whatever they are doing just for me or for no reason. There is always a selfish reason for everything somebody does. Either people do not have the consciousness to understand what that reason is, or they are trying to hide that reason from you in order to manipulate you.

I also made the decision to submit to a higher power. People said I just followed God because I only wanted to please him. If you look deeper, there's a reason that you want to please God and that you want to follow him. It's not for anyone else. The main reason is for you. I chose to submit to the scripture because of my belief that God was who he said he was in the scriptures. I wanted to be in a place where there was peace and comfort and submitting to scripture and believing in God was the best chance I had in accomplishing that desire. So, if I do any good for anybody, then I am not the one to be thanked. Rather, God should be thanked since it's from my desire to chase him that I do good on this earth.

Every decision had to benefit me in some form or fashion, or it was not a good decision. Thinking like this put me in a position to be successful inside the penitentiary. I remember my neighbor Art used to watch games with me on my television. I remember talking and laughing, eating breaks, and drinking a few *foxies*, which are a mixture of coffee and Kool-Aid.

One day, he got into it with this 135-pound white guy, and Art was about 270 pounds. The confrontation was over putting an extra laundry bag in the basket to get washed. Art was the laundry clerk, so he said no to the guy. Art let certain people put extra laundry bags in the basket, but you had to be cool with him in order to get the extra bag washed. The white guy refused and persisted in putting the extra laundry bag in the basket, and Art immediately told him to go to the bathroom—where they would not get caught—to fight. Art went to the bathroom, and the white guy went back to his bed area.

Now, this white guy had been incarcerated for over fifteen years, so he only knew one way to resolve conflict. He went back to his bed area to get a razor he had embedded into a toothbrush, but Art was so angry and arrogant that he did not even care about the guy getting a weapon.

There were about seven people that ran in the bathroom to see the fight. I remained at my bed area. Choosing to continue watching television was my decision because I told myself that the fight had nothing to do with me. If I was around the action, then they could make me a part of the action when the questions started. From past experience, the authorities usually always found out what happened through the people involved. Somebody usually told. They weren't going to include me because I wasn't going to be anywhere near the fight. Watching Art and the guy fight would not benefit me in any possible way, so I stayed at my bed area.

When it was all said and done, Art came out the bathroom needing over five hundred stitches from getting hit with the razor multiple times. The seven people who ran in to watch instantly became a part of the action and hit the smaller white guy with a mop handle trying to get him to release the blade. The white guy got a new charge, and four of the seven people in the bathroom also got charges for hitting the guy with the mop handle. Three of those seven were forced to either tell or get additional charges. They chose to tell. Art got stitched up and ended up going home at his regular release date. Everybody else got more time added to their sentences, except the one person pushing for the drama, which was Art.

I took a "hear no evil, see no evil, fear no evil" sort of mentality. There was a time that I would have been right in the middle of the scuffle, either instigating or being a part of the fight. That part of my character goes way back, to elementary school, when I was a young child. I always wanted to be involved. I thought it was cool and tough. Now being involved with the drama doesn't excite me. I guess you can say that as a child, I thought like a child, but now, as a man, I think like a man. The only reason I should be in a physical confrontation is if someone is trying to take my life, or the life of a family member, inside my household.

The most sense was to stay at my bed area and mind my own business. This was the decision that suited me the best. I would not have been fighting over a laundry bag going in the washer; therefore, I did not want to see someone else fighting over a laundry bag going into the washer.

Putting the burden on someone else's shoulders to obtain my success did not seem logical to me at all. I was vocal about what I stood for so it could not be misconstrued in any possible way. I told people that I had a son who needed his father present, and it served him better for me to be out there versus in prison. The majority of men incarcerated are fathers, so this always got me respect. When you take a stand for something, something goes out into the universe to allow that stand to be upheld.

You must apply the same aggression that got you incarcerated to your rehabilitation. It takes constant work to become a new individual, shedding those immature habits you have grown accustomed to during your years of existence. Shedding those habits is necessary to become a productive individual in prison and, in turn, becoming a productive member of society once released. There are decisions to be made on a daily basis inside prison, and if you do not make the correct ones, it's detrimental to your success as well as your life.

8

Forgiveness

FORGIVENESS IS ANOTHER barrier people face to becoming successful during prison. Forgiveness is a three-pronged process: asking for forgiveness, forgiving you, and forgiving others.

I hear so many times that people think the act of forgiving is for the other person, but forgiving is predominately for the person doing the forgiving. Forgiving is not saying you have forgotten what someone has done to you. Rather, it is saying you will not seek revenge or let that person control how you feel toward them. Just because you forgive someone does not mean you have to continue to be friends with that person or hang around that person. Forgiving is not condoning the behavior or denying the feeling that you feel about the particular behavior. You can tell if you have forgiven a person if you do not have any negative feelings arise when you hear that person's name or you see that person.

Understanding that you are a flawed individual will be the most important determining factor in being successful in the forgiveness process. As human beings, we are flawed by nature, and we are destined to make errors in life. When we make those errors, we look to be forgiven. Knowing that you need to be forgiven positions you in a place mentally to forgive yourself and others. This makes you more able to establish positive relationships because of your willingness to admit your wrongs and ask for forgiveness. People in general look at error as such a dirty act, and when it happens, nobody wants to take claim of it. This is the biggest mistake in your evolution because if you do not want to acknowledge your errors as errors, then you continue to commit them, causing you to be unsuccessful in your endeavors. Self-evaluation is always the most painful and most avoided act because it brings the most progress. It's easier to evaluate everybody else's wrong, but it's more difficult to evaluate your own. When you think about it, you cannot correct other people's wrongs. You only have the authority to correct your own wrongs. Punishment does not correct a person's wrong if that person does not want to correct it. Ultimately, it is up to the actual individuals to correct their wrongs.

In prison, you see people throughout the population struggling heavily with forgiveness, and it prevents them from going to the next level and becoming successful. There are an unfathomable number of people holding grudges. I realized the lack of forgiveness always stems from oneself. I made it a point not to let anyone occupy free space in my mind. I needed that space for powerful information to produce powerful behavior, so I could possess powerful results.

When I was on the streets, I felt as if my close friend committed an act of betrayal that could not be forgiven, causing me to move in on his life as a punishment. My immature mind felt this was what would ultimately teach him to do right and change once he ventured into the next life. I had no sense of forgiveness on any level. I never asked for forgiveness, because I rarely felt wrong, and when I did feel I might have been wrong, I justified and ignored my behavior. I never forgave myself because I believed I did not need to be forgiven, although people around me thought otherwise.

When you are alone at night, on your bunk, it is difficult to escape being real with yourself. I always desired to be real, even when I put myself in a situation to be in this hell. I just had a lack of knowledge about life and, ultimately, myself. I analyzed everything that had put me in prison, and the finger always pointed back to me. This was the time when life really started working for me. I found my error in everything that had happened to me, and I dedicated myself to correcting the errors in my thinking.

I was able to forgive everybody that might have done me wrong, because I could not help realizing all the wrong I had done to other people. I did not have time to hold grudges against anybody because of all the issues I had to address with myself. I asked God for forgiveness, I forgave myself, and in turn, forgave others. This put me in a premier place mentally since people who had committed trespasses against me did not know how to respond. They felt I would retaliate, but instead, I chose to separate. I got control of my life, and it felt powerful. I forgave people who told on me, I forgave people who stole from me, and I forgave people who abandoned me in my time of need. I learned from my experiences and avoided situations that produced the wrong results.

I looked at everything as something that I, myself, had done to cause my end result. If somebody told on me, then it was because I had done something worth getting told on for, and I needed to forgive myself for making a poor decision. When my drugs were stolen, I knew my friend was into robbing, but I was arrogant enough to think that he knew better than to rob me. I had to forgive myself for underestimating other people and being around an individual that was of a different mind-set than me. I did not hold any grudges against people who were cool with me when I was free, and they were nowhere to be found now that I had ten years to serve in prison. I realized I had made the decision to travel down this path, and I owned up to the results of my decisions. My situation would not change by being driven to pay people back who thought I was done. I would not let anger or hate consume me about people not being there. I took the stance that nobody owed me anything, but with that being said, I did not owe anybody anything either. A life with no hate will put you in place that allows you to establish relationships that are productive and positive.

If I failed, it was because of me. If I succeeded, it was also because of me. I was not going to give anyone the benefit to claim my failures because I was not going to give them the benefit to claim my successes. When you are the beneficiary for forgiveness, it always starts with yourself. The reason you are the main beneficiary of forgiveness is because if you are holding a grudge against someone, then the chances are high that the other person either does not know or does not care. Regardless, the main person affected by a grudge and un-forgiveness is you. That other person is going on with life as usual, and they are not bothered by your grudge. Being in this situation leaves no room to focus on anyone else because of the probability of you recidivating. All focus has to be on you and what you can do to better yourself. Counting the wrongs people have done to you is only a distraction to the main problem at hand—and that is you.

When you tend to hold grudges toward other people, the chances are you subject yourself to feeling guilty in certain situations, causing you to make bad decisions. When you feel as though you have done something wrong to somebody, and you have not forgiven yourself, your lack of forgiveness for yourself will keep you in prison.

I completely acknowledged my wrongs and asked the person for forgiveness. I forgave myself, and then I moved on. My freedom was not contingent upon the other person agreeing to forgive me but contingent on whether I was willing to forgive myself.

I asked my son to forgive me for making the decisions that put me in prison and separated us. Once I asked for forgiveness, and I forgave myself, I was able to move with power in our relationship.

People hold you hostage when they feel you are having trouble forgiving yourself, and I did not want to be a person held hostage by something in my past that I had already addressed. Forgiveness is mandatory to making it to the next level in life. I always talked about what I was doing because that dictated where I was going. Forgiveness is for you, and the first to forgive before you extend forgiveness to others is yourself.

9

Time Is Valuable

THE TWENTY-FOUR HOURS the president of the United States of America has every day are the same twenty-four hours a person who is incarcerated has as well. Time is the most valuable asset known to mankind; it is the only thing that cannot be replaced. You can replace or repair everything else in your life—your car, your house, your money, or your significant other. Time cannot be replaced. Once it's gone, it's gone. The successful people inside prison, and in the world, maximize their time to the fullest because they understand its value. Understanding who you are and what success means to you is only half the battle. You must then invest the time to accomplish it. Success is costly, and the only asset that can pay for it is time.

My grandmother is eighty-three years old, and I recall, not too long ago, when she had to bury the last of her siblings. She has buried her mother, father, brothers, aunts, uncles, cousins, and friends, and finally, she saw her sister buried.

I called Grandma with a voice of comfort and sincerity to try to help her through this most difficult time in her life. She and her sister had been very close.

With a firm and convinced tone, Grandma said, "Carlos, this is life, and longevity comes with a price. With longevity, you will have to experience heartache and pain by separating from the people that you love, because they were not given the opportunity to continue."

Those words were so profound that I sat back and marveled at my grand-mother's wisdom.

Time is not free. It is paid for by the suffering we automatically go through the longer we are here on this earth. If we have to pay for time with our heartache and pain, then why do we trade our time in exchange for dead relationships? Why do we trade our time in exchange for insignificant things? Why do we trade our time in exchange for going in and out of prison? If you understand the value of time, you break the bars in any prison that exists in this world. Time should be spent on becoming the person you were put here to be.

I always heard people throughout the prison say, "Do your time, and don't let the time do you." This saying means that during your time in prison, take care of yourself, and do not let the time make you crazy to the point that it diminishes your health and your appearance.

I was convinced I had to be productive with my time, because I knew it was valuable, and I did not want to take it for granted. I worked on changing the individual I had been to become an individual I wanted to be. I viewed prison as any situation I had encountered in my past. I wanted to be victorious.

The first five years of my sentence, I was not able to get into any college courses or vocational training, so I worked heavily on my spirit and my body. I studied scripture to get a new understanding on life and gain the wisdom necessary to be successful in my everyday life. This started my transformation. I also tuned in to *The Potter's House* and watched T. D. Jakes for a better understanding on this new way of living. If I was going to be positive, then I needed to saturate my mind with positive information, and what was more positive than scripture? This dedication consumed about three hours of my day.

I applied the scripture to my life and began practicing this new way of thinking. Being productive meant becoming a better individual so I could enjoy all the spoils in life. You feel when you are becoming better because you can see yourself making different decisions, and you find yourself in situations that are more prosperous.

I rapped before I was incarcerated, so I continued trying to create an option for myself when I got released. Everything was focused on the end—my release date. During the ten years, I wrote books and books of rhymes. This gave me an accomplished feeling because I was creating something from scratch. When you are productive, it combats the negative feelings you encounter while going through this experience.

I recall feeling as if there was not enough time in the day, even while I was incarcerated. This was because my mind was evolving and becoming free, and this ultimately freed my body as well.

I made sure I exercised at a high level to be as healthy as possible. Plus, I thought about how it would be with women when I was released. When you are away from women for so long, this is always a part of your thoughts. I wanted to create a body women would be all over, so when I thought about it, I worked even harder. Even though it was a bit simpleminded, in its truest form, this was still productive activity, and I was improving on the person that I was before incarceration.

I was obsessed with improvement on all levels. I was not going to be the dude who slept the majority of the day with hopes that, when I woke up, the time would be over. Everybody who did, woke up unprepared on their release date, and they went home only to recidivate and sleep some more on the same bunk they had left.

I made sure I wrote my son once a week with the inmates' free envelopes for my whole time. I did not want him thinking I'd forgotten about him. Even when he was only three years old, I still took time out of my day to write him. I wrote him in all capital letters, and I skipped lines so his mother could read along with him during father-and-son time. This helped him stay connected to me, and it helped him learn how to read. I got people to draw artwork to send to him. I also went to the commissary on special occasions such as holidays or birthdays and bought him fifteen dollars' worth of candy and used five dollars to mail the candy home to him. Instead of just a letter in the mail, all the times, on those special occasions throughout the year, he got the letter and a box full of candy. Establishing a positive relationship with my son was a part of my success that I wanted to create in my future. Time is time, and I was using it to build myself a future that I was satisfied with, without a shadow of a doubt.

I got involved in any program that supported my idea of success. I was intentional and deliberate with what I participated in. I took part in an Aunt Mary's Storybook Telling program, which was a program that allowed us to choose between a variety of children's books. They gave us a tape to record on while reading the book to our child. They then paid the postage and sent the book and the tape home to the child. I reported to this program every month. My time had to reflect who I was becoming, not who I had been, and I was serious about what I chose to do during my bid.

I was serious about everything the prison had to offer. After all, I was a hustler, and a hustler always looks to come out on top in whatever he or she does. That was my way of thinking.

I remember that, for ten years, I filled out kites every six months to get my teeth cleaned. Dental work cost money, so I wanted it, because it had value. I was not going to be a dude who did nothing during his time incarcerated only to come back and continue paying somebody's salary. I did not like being bamboozled, and I felt I had been. But I was not going to stay bamboozled. I was making choices that were going to turn the tables around in my life.

The people I hung with supported my idea of success. If someone was going in a direction that read "penitentiary," I did not give him much time. There are people to spend five days with or five minutes with, but you have to know the difference. The reason I was around people for only five minutes was to either speak to them about why this new way of thinking was necessary, or I was trying to learn from their errors and failures so I did not commit the same ones. I was in different conversations about my ideology, and people always doubted my theory that before change can be seen externally, change must be done internally. If you wanted to be successful once you got released, you had to be successful while you were incarcerated.

Change starts within—first within yourself and then within your current situation. Waiting for change to come was not a part of my mentality. I was determined to go and make change. The first and most important change I made was within me by attacking the way I lived my life and made my decisions. If you squander your most valuable asset, then you have no choice but being destitute and poor. I refused to be either because I maximized my time. The last five years of my time, I got involved in the college program for business management and also administrative office technology for vocational training.

I remember when a correctional officer told me that because I was in prison, he obtained enough overtime pay to purchase a motorcycle for the summer. He thanked me for making a decision to be in prison. He said that my failure was his success. Of course, I had to thank him as well for being an honest taxpaying citizen, and because of that, I was able to get my teeth cleaned twice a year and take advantage of the college credits worth about $230 per credit. I made sure I got all 140 credits offered as well. I also made sure that I actually learned the material so I could apply the knowledge once I was released to capture my idea of success. I explained to him that it was as if we were helping each other. There were some people that took the college courses just to avoid being classified in the kitchen, but I took these courses to build my future.

I remember when dudes tried to copy off my tests because I scored very high on my tests. I always told them to beat it and manage their time better. While they played dominoes and cards in the yard, I learned the material. I would not let somebody who squandered his time benefit off me. I was able to get a good grasp on the material taught by the college professors, and with it, my confidence grew in my ability to obtain that successful life I had envisioned.

To be in college, I also had to make sure I was not absent from any classes. People were removed from college because they could not stay out of segregation. If you cannot do what it takes to achieve your goals while you are incarcerated, then there is no way that you will be able to achieve your goals once you get released. I could not capitalize on my time in segregation, and therefore, it was not the place for my presence to occupy. I made this time count because it was valuable, and if I possessed the most valuable asset known to mankind, then I had value. Putting myself in situations like prison was not my idea of maximizing my time. I put everything in place to never experience this again.

After I graduated from college with a certificate in business management, I immediately did my final year of my incarceration in vocational training for administrative office technology.

The secret to being successful in prison is maximizing your time and not leaving any parts of your day unaccounted for. Every action has to support your mission. You have to focus on everything you partake of. If you are not together, then everyone you want to help cannot be helped because you are not taken care of mentally, physically, and spiritually. Accomplishing this task all starts with you. It all starts within. This mentality will have you living in a prison without bars.

Conclusion

THE RECIDIVISM RATE decreasing is not solely contingent on whether there are enough opportunities in society for restored citizens. The major barrier for individuals reentering society after incarceration is the individual. I'm not saying there will be no other challenges, because there are challenges with everything in life—especially things that are important. If there is no enemy within, the enemy outside can do you no harm, which means, in spite of the many challenges that you encounter once released, none of these challenges are too great to overcome as long as you have not made yourself your own worst enemy and your biggest barrier. Conquering the enemy within takes time and commitment. Time is the most valuable asset, and you must capitalize on every minute of the day. Possessing this most valuable asset means you are a valuable individual. It does not matter if you are incarcerated. Time still ticks the same way that it ticks for the president of the United States.

Prison without Bars discusses living a life in prison that mimics the same disciplines it takes to be successful once released. This book talks about utilizing your time to condition your mind, spirit, and body in a way that does not have incarceration on its horizon. To be truly free, you must first be free in your mind, and then it is only a matter of time before your body follows. Being able to establish positive relationships is imperative to your success in prison as well as in life.

The first positive relationship that must be established is your relationship with yourself. Before you start the journey of redesigning yourself in a way that puts you in the most desirable situations, you must first do a self-evaluation. What is your idea of success? Where do you want to be in life? What is your idea of an enriched life? Who do you want to share your life with while on this earth? Once you find the honest answers for those questions, then your journey begins.

I was nineteen years old, with a three-month-old child, and I had to do a ten-year prison sentence. I came to the conclusion that prison was not my idea of success, and I was adamant about evolving from any mentality that supported more prison time. My success started in prison with doing time in a way that warranted respect. Ultimately, I was able to build on a solid foundation once I got released from prison eight years ago, in August 2007. Despite being released with attempted murder and drug and gun cases on my jacket, I was able to secure employment within the first few weeks of my release. This was two months before the great recession. I was employed for minimum wage, but I was able to establish my work history and, in turn, my life.

The growth I accomplished in prison was what put me in a position to be successful. I gained custody of my son, who was ten years old, from his mother because she wanted me to raise him to be a man, and she trusted me with our son because of what I had accomplished while incarcerated. He is emulating the man I am now, not the man I was, because he does not know that man. I am confident that he will face his own struggles, but he will not duplicate mine.

I met and married my wife, and we later founded the Starts Within Organization to assist people while incarcerated in becoming who they need to be, *prerelease*, so they do not recidivate. Our organization is well respected by governmental agencies as well as other agencies in the state of Ohio. We established positive relationships with the Ohio Department of Rehabilitation and Correction, CSEA, Franklin County courts, Franklin County Child Services, Action for Children, Adult Parole Authority, and the Ohio Commission on Fatherhood, just to name a few. It is a joy to watch the Cleveland Browns every week and have family vacations on cruises to the Bahamas. When I was on the streets, I never thought this life was possible. My quality of life is at an all-time high, and I appreciate every second. Life is best when made simple, and I have made it simple.

Change starts with you and with knowing you can make a difference in the world. People who are incarcerated are gifted individuals, but society attempts to beat them down to the point that they believe the nonsense. Once we find our way, the sky is the limit, and anything is possible. The communities and the nation will be different because of it. The time is now to change the world by changing yourself. Go be great, live without limitations, and live a life without bars.

About the Author

AT AGE THIRTEEN, Carlos Christian became involved in the drug trade—eventually leading to a ten-year prison sentence. He was incarcerated at the Marion Correctional Institution in Marion, Ohio, from age nineteen to twenty-nine. During his sentence, Christian was dedicated to his rehabilitation and becoming a positive role model. He graduated from Marion Technical College majoring in business management, with a 3.83 GPA. In addition, he successfully completed an Administrative Office Technology vocational program. Upon his release, Christian had support from his friends, family, and a case manager. After he obtained employment, Christian relocated to Columbus, where he became a homeowner, gained custody of his son, and began to mentor incarcerated individuals in penitentiaries and county jails.

During Christian's prison sentence, he realized that he had seen more individuals being released from prison and returning than he had of individuals being released from prison and going on to lead positive lives in the community. Christian founded the Starts Within Organization (SWO) in 2011 because of his determination to help currently incarcerated men build the same solid foundation—pre-and post-release—that he was able to build.

SWO is based on the principal that individuals must start within themselves and start within their current situations. SWO is a nonprofit organization that combats the alarming recidivism rate that hinders the growth of communities across the nation. By strategically placing these men in career fields related to their skills and knowledge, SWO is working toward the goal of becoming the organization that offers a model reentry program in the nation.

Christian began his work with Action for Children in 2010 as a facilitator for TAPP; Father Factor. Using the Father Factor curriculum, he has helped nearly four hundred fathers across central Ohio. TAPP; Father Factor is about building better parent-child relationships and opening doors to positive communication between coparents. As a father himself, Christian knows how impactful fatherhood can be. He understands how a father's role within a family can positively or negatively affect children's social and emotional development. Christian consistently strives for excellence when working with fathers because he knows that by bettering families, we are bettering the community as a whole.

"12-31-99"

My father would drive for six hours to pick up my son from his mother and come to the institution throughout the year. This played a major role in my success.

My Child and I Day June 28th 2003 Marion Correctional Institution.

I was determined to be a good dad no matter what the circumstances were.

Marion Technical College Graduation 2006

Carlos Jr. Westerville High Graduation 2015

Breaking the cycle!

This was a proud dad moment.

Cleveland Browns game 2015

Carnival Cruise Bahamas July 4th, 2014. To go from being right next door to hell to having a slice of Heaven is a beautiful feeling!

Made in the USA
Middletown, DE
02 November 2015